IN THE RHYTHM OF THE NEEDLES
THERE IS MUSIC FOR THE SOUL.

OLD SAMPLER

The simple act of knitting, of counting stitches and rows,
losing oneself in the rhythm of pattern repeats, and the
joy of watching a lovely piece of handiwork emerge,
helps release tension and allows one to forget,
if only for a moment, the realities of life.

Especially for

_____

From

_____

Date

_____

© 2011 by Barbour Publishing, Inc.

Written and compiled by Anne C. Watkins in association with Snapdragon Editorial Group℠, Tulsa, OK.

ISBN 978-1-61626-224-2

Published by Barbour Publishing, Inc., P.O. Box 719, Uhrichsville, Ohio 44683, www.barbourbooks.com

Our mission is to publish and distribute inspirational products offering exceptional value and biblical encouragement to the masses.

Printed in China.

Simple Tips & Inspiration
for Knitters

BARBOUR
PUBLISHING

KNITTING IS AS MUCH ABOUT THE JOURNEY
AS IT IS ABOUT THE DESTINATION.

WHEN CHANGING COLOR IN A STRIPED PIECE, START THE NEW COLOR AT THE BEGINNING OF A PURL ROW.

Some needles don't have the sizes marked or printed on them. Determine the size with a needle gauge tool, and using a fine-tipped permanent marker, write the size on the knob at the end of the needle or directly on the needle body.

THE LARGER THE NEEDLE, THE LARGER THE COMPLETED STITCH WILL BE.

Knitting is a common thread in some popular fiction, such as *The Friday Night Knitting Club* by Kate Jacobs, *The House on Blossom Street* by Debbie Macomber, and *The Knitting Circle* by Ann Hood.

IF YOU DISLIKE SEWING SEAMS WITH A NEEDLE, TRY USING A CROCHET HOOK IN THE APPROPRIATE SIZE AND SLIP-STITCHING THE SEAMS TOGETHER.

When knitting a large project like an afghan or a bulky sweater, save wear and tear on your hands by knitting back and forth on a long circular needle. This allows the weight of the work to rest on your lap, rather than on the straight needles you're holding.

Amaze your non-knitting friends and family by casually working a sock on double-pointed needles. All those pointy ends sticking out while you click away will make you look incredibly mysterious and cool. (Hint: Save the heel turning for alone time.)

LOVE, JOY, PEACE, KNITTING.

UNKNOWN

The good thing about knitting is that there are almost as many ways of doing things as there are knitters. Your technique might not match that of another knitter, but as long as the finished stitches are correct, that's all that matters.

KNITTING GENERALLY TAKES
LESS YARN FOR A COMPARABLY
SIZED PROJECT THAN CROCHETING.

WHILE THERE ARE TOO MANY FANCY
STITCHES TO COUNT, JUST TWO,
THE LOWLY KNIT AND PURL STITCHES,
FORM THE BASIS FOR THEM ALL.

Perfect your steek technique on a swatch before sinking those scissors into the item in which you've just invested so many precious hours knitting.

Sturdy drumstick bags make excellent storage receptacles for knitting needles. The narrow zippered bags feature roomy inside pockets and are made from materials like coated nylon or cordura. Check with local music stores or online music supply sites for prices and availability.

DON'T HAVE A POINT PROTECTOR? DOUBLED OR TRIPLED BULKY RUBBER BANDS ROLLED ONTO THE ENDS OF THE NEEDLES WILL HELP KEEP YOUR WORK FROM SLIPPING OFF.

Purchase inexpensive three-ring binders and a supply of clear sheet protectors. These are handy for storing and organizing your knitting patterns or favorite knitting articles.

ASIDE FROM METAL AND CARVED, POLISHED WOOD, SOME ANTIQUE KNITTING NEEDLES WERE MADE FROM IVORY TUSKS, TORTOISE SHELLS, THIN PIECES OF WIRE, OR FEATHER QUILLS.

IN A PINCH, CHOPSTICKS, PENCILS, OR BAMBOO SKEWERS MAKE FINE SUBSTITUTE NEEDLES.

Make it your ambition to lead a quiet life,
to mind your own business and to work with your hands.

1 THESSALONIANS 4:11

COTTON AND SILK WERE TWO OF
THE EARLIEST MATERIALS
USED FOR KNITTING.

Large, clean, plastic coffee containers make excellent yarn ball holders. Pop your ball of yarn inside, set it beside your chair, and knit away. No more chasing that wily ball of yarn across the floor. (This is also a wonderful excuse to drink lots of coffee.)

TRANSFORM YOUR COLLECTION OF
SWATCHES INTO CHEERFUL PATCHWORK
BLANKETS, FUNKY SCARVES, OR THE
FRONT PANELS OF A VEST.

You can commune with other knitting enthusiasts by attending knitting retreats, conventions, or taking a craft cruise. Search for details on the Internet or inside the pages of your favorite knitting publications.

PRACTICE NEW STITCHES ON SMALL PROJECTS LIKE SCARVES, DISHCLOTHS, OR DOLL BLANKETS. BY THE TIME YOU'VE FINISHED THE PROJECT, YOU'LL HAVE MASTERED THE STITCH AND COMPLETED A NIFTY GIFT TO SHARE WITH YOUR FAVORITE KNIT-LOVER.

Use a lifeline when knitting lace by threading a tapestry needle with a length of yarn and running it through a row of simple stitches, like the purl row in feather-and-fan. This makes ripping out and redoing yarn-overs and decreases much less stressful.

IF YOUR STITCHES KEEP SLIPPING OFF METAL NEEDLES, TRY SWITCHING TO WOODEN, BAMBOO, OR PLASTIC NEEDLES, WHICH PROVIDE A LITTLE MORE GRIP.

Invest in a supply of zip-top plastic bags in a variety of sizes. The largest bags can hold sweater parts or afghan blocks, while smaller bags keep tools and gadgets neatly corralled and visible.

Plain yarn can be dyed with unsweetened powdered drink mixes and a splash of vinegar. The mixes are available in a rainbow of colors, including purple, blue, red, yellow, and green. You can also use food coloring or Easter egg dyes. Follow package directions.

KNITTING IS VERY CONDUCIVE TO THOUGHT.
IT IS NICE TO KNIT AWHILE, PUT DOWN
THE NEEDLES, WRITE AWHILE, THEN TAKE
UP THE SOCK AGAIN.

DOROTHY DAY

A DOUBLE-POINTED NEEDLE WITH A POINT PROTECTOR ON EACH END MAKES A HANDY STITCH HOLDER FOR SMALL PROJECTS.

If you like to knit in bed but don't want the light to disturb your partner, illuminate your work by using a small reading light. The ones with the bendy, adjustable necks are convenient and inexpensive.

WORKING WITH DARK YARNS CAN BE A STRAIN ON THE EYES. TURN UP THE ROOM LIGHTS OR TRY ONE OF THE CONVENIENT KNITTING LIGHTS YOU WEAR AROUND YOUR NECK.

When weaving yarn ends into the finished piece, use a tapestry needle or small crochet hook to draw the yarn through a few stitches in one direction. Then run it in the opposite direction for a few stitches. This will keep it from coming loose.

When giving a knitted gift, snip the care information from the yarn label and attach it to a pretty card. Slip the card into an envelope and include it with the item. This way the recipient will know how to properly care for their new handcrafted treasure.

First Lady Eleanor Roosevelt inspired knitters around the country to knit and contribute items to benefit soldiers serving in World War II. Photographs of Mrs. Roosevelt knitting, or with knitting bag in hand, frequently appeared in national newspapers and magazines.

To avoid unpleasant interruptions, always read through a new pattern before you cast on your first stitch. This way you won't be surprised if you come across an unfamiliar term or direction.

Add a cheerful splash of color to any room by rolling leftover yarn into balls and piling them into a pretty basket or large clear glass container. Then just tuck it into a corner or set it out on a dresser or coffee table.

If your bound-off edges always end up too tight, next time try using a larger needle to bind off. This will make the edge a bit looser and provide more give.

KNIT YOUR HEARTS
WITH AN UNSLIPPING KNOT.

WILLIAM SHAKESPEARE

Musk ox wool, or *qiviut* (pronounced "kiv-ee-ute"), is said to be eight times warmer than regular wool. Qiviut yarn is spun from the super-soft undercoat shed by the musk ox and doesn't shrink when washed, is hypoallergenic, and produces an extraordinarily soft fabric.

IF YOU WANT A SNUGGER FINISHED EDGE, SAY FOR A NECKLINE, TRY BINDING OFF WITH A SMALLER-SIZED NEEDLE THAN YOU USED FOR THE BODY OF THE GARMENT.

Queen Victoria's love of knitting inspired many of her subjects to take up their needles. However, items rich with elaborate lace stitches and meticulous detail were often knitted with no formal patterns. Due to the heightened interest, England's first knitting pattern books were published during the Victorian era (1837–1901).

WHEN KNITTING 2X2 RIBBING IN THE ROUND, START BY CASTING ON AN AMOUNT DIVISIBLE BY FOUR. CAST ON A NUMBER DIVISIBLE BY TWO FOR 1X1 RIBBING. THIS WAY YOUR RIBBING COMES OUT EVEN WHERE THE NEXT ROUND BEGINS.

There's nothing quite like taking a shapeless ball of yarn and a couple of knitting needles and watching a sweater emerge from your fingertips. It's sort of like giving birth, but less painful.

ANGORA WOOL COMES FROM THE SOFT FUR OF ANGORA RABBITS. ANGORA GOATS PRODUCE MOHAIR.

When knitting a garment in the round, it's a good idea to knit your gauge swatch in the round, too. This way you can see how the yarn and the stitches will look when worked in the round.

WORK A SWATCH OR TWO IN THE SAME STITCH YOU'LL BE USING FOR THE PATTERN.

WHEN KNITTING A LACE STITCH ON A LONG PATTERN ROW, USE A STITCH MARKER AFTER EVERY PATTERN REPEAT.
THIS WAY IF YOU MESS UP, YOU WON'T HAVE TO RIP OUT THE WHOLE ROW, BUT JUST BACK TO THE MARKER.

Well-done work has its own reward.

PROVERBS 12:14 MSG

Wedding ring shawls are delicate, lightweight lace shawls that are knit at such a fine gauge they can be drawn through a wedding ring.

IF THE TERMS SSK, K2TOG, AND TURN THE HEEL MAKE PERFECT SENSE TO YOU, YOU MUST BE A KNITTER.

WHEN YOU'RE WORKING WITH DOUBLE-POINTED NEEDLES, USE ONE NEEDLE TO HOLD ALL THE CAST ON STITCHES. THEN DIVIDE THE STITCHES BETWEEN THE NEEDLES PER THE PATTERN INSTRUCTIONS.

Don't be afraid to try a pattern that is flagged as experienced or difficult. What may be difficult for someone else might be easy for you. And if it doesn't work out, just frog the whole thing, roll the yarn into a ball, and start something else.

KEEP A SMALL CROCHET HOOK HANDY FOR PICKING UP DROPPED STITCHES.

Count your completed cast on stitches by twos. This makes counting large numbers of stitches faster and easier, especially if you're a new knitter and find it difficult to keep an accurate count during the casting on process.

When working on your first few knitted projects, it's a good idea to stop and count your stitches after every row. Keeping an accurate stitch count helps assure the satisfactory completion of your project.

SOMETIMES IT'S EASIER TO KNIT DIRECTLY FROM A DISCARDED PIECE THAN TO RIP THE WHOLE THING APART AND ROLL IT INTO A BALL.

THE SMALL FONT USED FOR
SOME PATTERNS MAKES THEM
DIFFICULT TO READ. ENLARGE THE
PATTERNS ON YOUR PRINTER TO
MAKE THEM EASIER ON THE EYES.

It took me years and years of trial efforts to work out that there is absolutely no knitting triumph I can achieve that my husband will think is worth being woken up for.

STEPHANIE PEARL-MCPHEE

A FISHING TACKLE BOX WITH ALL ITS DIFFERENT-SIZED COMPARTMENTS MAKES A SUPER KNITTING NOTIONS CONTAINER. SOME MODELS EVEN FEATURE RECONFIGURABLE DIVIDERS.

Use a three-ring binder and clear sheet protectors to contain those pesky circular needles with their loopy cables. You can write the needle sizes directly on the sheet protectors or use stick-on labels.

Knit a soft, snuggly comfort, prayer,
or friendship shawl for someone going
through a tough time. Each time it is worn,
the recipient will be surrounded by the love
and prayers knit into each stitch.

IF YOU KNOW THAT WIP STANDS FOR WORK IN PROGRESS, YOU MUST BE A KNITTER. IF YOUR WIPS ARE TAKING OVER YOUR HOUSE, THERE'S NO DOUBT ABOUT IT; YOU DEFINITELY ARE A KNITTER.

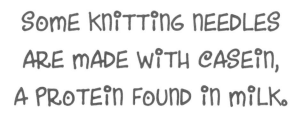

SOME KNITTING NEEDLES
ARE MADE WITH CASEIN,
A PROTEIN FOUND IN MILK.

Save your prescription medicine bottles and use them to hold stitch markers, yarn needles, point protectors, and other small knitting accessories. Clean the bottles thoroughly, and remove the labels before repurposing them for your knitting gear.

Share your tried and true knitting tricks with a new knitter. They'll benefit from your hard-earned wisdom, and you'll have helped someone learn to love knitting just as much as you do.

YOU CAN SUBSTITUTE A DOUBLE-POINTED
NEEDLE OR A SMALL CROCHET HOOK
FOR A CABLE NEEDLE.

BOBBY PINS MAKE DANDY STITCH MARKERS. YOU CAN ALSO USE BOBBY PINS TO HOLD SEAMS TOGETHER BEFORE STITCHING.

I like making a piece of string into something I can wear.

UNKNOWN

Ladders are those annoying loose stitches that sometimes show up between your last stitch from one double-pointed needle and your first stitch from the next needle. One way to prevent them is by tugging the yarn tight before and after the first stitch on the new needle.

AN HOUR OF KNITTING IS CHEAPER
THAN AN HOUR OF THERAPY.

IF YOU DON'T HAVE ACCESS TO A COMPUTER AND PRINTER TO ENLARGE YOUR KNITTING PATTERNS, PURCHASE A PAGE-SIZED MAGNIFIER SHEET AND POSITION IT OVER THE PATTERN.

Large safety pins make great holders for stitch markers. As long as the pin isn't too heavy, you can attach it to the bottom of your project to keep extra markers handy.

Flat knitting is produced by working back and forth in rows, turning the work after each row. Circular knitting is knitting in the round, either by using double-pointed needles or one or more circular needles.

THE DYE LOT NUMBER ON A YARN LABEL INDICATES THAT ALL YARNS BEARING THAT LOT NUMBER WERE DYED IN THE SAME VAT AT THE SAME TIME. ALWAYS PURCHASE ENOUGH YARN IN THE SAME DYE LOT NUMBER TO ENSURE A UNIFORM COLOR IN YOUR FINISHED WORK.

If you find yourself becoming frustrated, give yourself permission to put down your knitting and take a break. Doing something else for a while allows your brain to reset and gives you a new perspective. But don't rush yourself; everything will still be there when you get back.

WHEN LEARNING TO KNIT LACE, WORK ON
WOOD, PLASTIC, OR BAMBOO NEEDLES,
WHICH PROVIDE MORE TRACTION AND KEEP
THE STITCHES FROM SLIDING
OFF THE ENDS.

ORPHAN SOCKS ARE WHAT YOU GET WHEN
YOU KNIT ONLY ONE OF A PAIR.

The Lord your God will bless you in all your harvest and in all the work of your hands, and your joy will be complete.

DEUTERONOMY 16:15

When you've finished knitting for the day, stop at the end of a row. Stopping in the middle of a row sometimes results in confusion or dropped stitches when you take up the work again.

TINK IS KNIT SPELLED BACKWARD AND IS
WHAT YOU DO WHEN YOU UNKNIT YOUR WORK
ONE STITCH AT A TIME BACK THROUGH A
ROW (OR ROWS) SO YOU CAN FIX
A MISTAKE.

SLIP YOUR SKEIN OF WORKING
YARN INSIDE A KNEE-HIGH NYLON
STOCKING TO KEEP IT CLEAN AND
FREE FROM TANGLING.

Aran sweaters are named for the Aran Islands, which are located off Ireland's west coast. Also called fisherman sweaters, they typically feature cables and other intricate designs. Traditional Aran sweaters are tightly knit from cream-colored, lanolin-rich wool, which makes them somewhat water resistant and very warm.

Casting stitches onto a circular needle can be clumsy business. Try casting on using a straight needle and then transfer the cast on stitches from the straight needle to the circular. Proceed per pattern instructions.

IF YOU KNOW THAT THE WORD FROG DOESN'T ALWAYS REFER TO AN AMPHIBIOUS CREATURE, YOU ARE A KNITTER. THIS BIT OF KNITTING SLANG COMES FROM THE ACT OF RIPPING OUT STITCHES, AS IN "RIP IT; RIP IT; RIP IT."

KNITTING PATTERNS WERE ONCE COMMONLY CALLED "RECIPES;" A FEW MODERN KNITTERS STILL REFER TO THEIR PATTERNS AS RECIPES.

Lend a hand to a beginner stumbling over an unfamiliar stitch or newly attempted technique. While you're teaching, be open-minded to their comments and movements. You may discover a grace in their awkwardness that triggers a new way of thinking for you.

Touch a life by donating knitted items to charities. For a list of agencies or worthy causes, plug the words *charity knitting* into your favorite Internet search engine. Follow the guidelines; most charities will have a list of specific items, materials, or patterns required.

IF THE KNITTER IS WEARY, THE BABY WILL HAVE NO NEW BONNET.

IRISH PROVERB

THROWERS ARE THOSE WHO KNIT ENGLISH-STYLE, OR WITH THE WORKING YARN HELD IN THE RIGHT HAND. PICKERS ARE CONTINENTAL-STYLE KNITTERS, WHO HOLD THE WORKING YARN IN THEIR LEFT HAND.

Sock monkey toys, with their characteristic red mouths, are popular folk art items. Some of the earliest American examples were made from the former Nelson Knitting Company's machine-knitted socks. Modern sock monkeys are a wilder, more colorful bunch, with some fanciful monkeys sporting argyle, striped, or tie-dyed sock designs.

Plarn is yarn made of narrow strips cut from plastic shopping bags and tied together into lengths. It can be knitted into rugs, toys, tote bags, and other durable items.

RECYCLED PLASTIC SODA BOTTLES ARE USED IN SOME YARN BLENDS.

A ply is a single spun, twisted strand of fiber. Twisting the plied strands together results in multi-plied yarns, such as 2-ply, 3-ply, or 4-ply yarns. Yarns can be plied in numerous configurations, giving them different appearances and textures.

The first time you encounter a sock pattern, the instructions look like a jumbled mass of confusion, especially that turning the heel business. Take your time and believe what the pattern tells you. Before you know it, you'll end up with something that looks surprisingly sock-like!

MAKE SURE YOUR YARN IS IN FRONT OF THE NEEDLES WHEN YOU MAKE A PURL STITCH.

PICKING UP STITCHES IS EASY IF YOU USE
A SMALL CROCHET HOOK TO PULL THE YARN
LOOP THROUGH AND PLACE IT ON YOUR NEEDLE.

Take a little time to familiarize yourself with knitting abbreviations. That way you won't be stumped when the pattern says to sl 1, k9, sl 1, k1, psso, k1, turn.

AS i GET OLDER,
i JUST PREFER TO KNIT.

TRACEY ULLMAN

ONCE YOU GET THE HANG OF IT,
YOU CAN KNIT, WATCH TELEVISION,
AND HELP WITH HOMEWORK ALL
AT THE SAME TIME.

Guinness Book of World Records holder Miriam Tegels is the fastest knitter in the world. The Netherlands resident set the speed record in 2006 by knitting 118 stitches in one minute.

One of the awesome things about knitting is its portability. Grab your knitting bag as you head out the door and transform all that time spent in waiting rooms, on the subway, or in line at the post office into socks, baby blankets, or sweaters.

DOUBLE-POINTED NEEDLES ARE THE OLDEST KNOWN TYPE OF KNITTING NEEDLES.

A selection of oil paintings dating from the fourteenth century pictures the Virgin Mary knitting on double-pointed needles. The paintings are commonly referred to as the Knitting Madonnas.

KEEP A NEEDLE GAUGE TOOL IN YOUR KNITTING BAG FOR THOSE TIMES YOU CAN'T REMEMBER WHAT SIZE YOUR UNMARKED NEEDLES ARE. THE GAUGES ARE PARTICULARLY HANDY FOR DOUBLE-POINTED NEEDLES.

Garter stitch is what you get by knitting every row back and forth. Stockinette stitch results from knitting one row and then purling the next.

BEFORE KNITTING A GIFT FROM WOOL OR WOOL-BLEND YARN, CHECK TO MAKE SURE THE RECIPIENT ISN'T ALLERGIC TO WOOL.

IF THE THOUGHT OF KNITTING SOCKS ON DOUBLE-POINTED NEEDLES MAKES YOU BREAK OUT IN HIVES, RELAX.
SOCKS KNITTED FLAT ON TWO STRAIGHT NEEDLES AND THEN SEAMED UP LOOK AND FEEL JUST AS NICE.

To enjoy your work and to accept your lot in life—
this is indeed a gift from God.

ECCLESIASTES 5:19 NLT

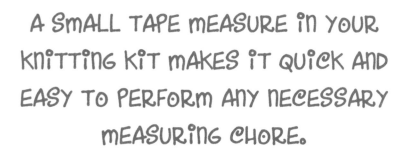

A SMALL TAPE MEASURE IN YOUR KNITTING KIT MAKES IT QUICK AND EASY TO PERFORM ANY NECESSARY MEASURING CHORE.

Cable needles hold the stitches you slip off the needle so you can knit, or twist, the first part of the cable. The slipped-off stitches are then worked from the cable needle, which is held either in front of the work or behind, depending upon the particular cable stitch.

USE A HIGHLIGHTER TO MARK YOUR PLACE IN THE PATTERN. THE INK COLOR SHOWS YOU WHERE YOU ARE, BUT IS TRANSLUCENT SO YOU CAN STILL READ THE DIRECTIONS.

A pull skein of yarn can be worked in two different ways. Pull the yarn end out from the center and knit as directed, or remove the paper label and work from the outside by grasping the loose end and unwinding the yarn as you go.

Not all wool yarns shrink or felt;
some can be machine washed and dried.
Check the yarn label and follow
the cleaning instructions.

TOSS SOME FINGERNAIL CLIPPERS INTO YOUR KNITTING KIT. THEY MAKE GREAT YARN CUTTERS AND TAKE UP LESS ROOM THAN A PAIR OF SCISSORS.

STORE YOUR YARN STASH IN A HANGING SHOE HOLDER. THE OPEN FRONTS ALLOW FOR QUICK ACCESS WHILE PROTECTING THE YARN FROM DUST OR WEAR.

Fair Isle and stranded knitting are basically the same thing, but traditional Fair Isle knitting incorporates just two colors per row. In both Fair Isle and stranded knitting, the yarn color not in use is carried loosely across the back of the work until needed.

Put together a knitting kit for each project
and store it with your work in progress.
Necessary items include stitch markers,
row counters, small crochet hook, tape measure
or ruler, yarn needle, scissors or fingernail
clippers, point protectors, pencil, and note pad.

KNiTTiNG CONTRiBUTES
TO GLOBAL WARMiNG.

HEDDY PARKER

Pop a small keychain flashlight in with your knitting gear for the times you need a little extra illumination on the stitches or printed pattern. You can also use it to find your way through a dark room if the power unexpectedly goes out.

If you get lost mid-row and can't remember which way you were going, look at the stitches. The working yarn will be attached to the last stitch you knitted (or purled) and that needle should be in your right hand. Switch hands if necessary and you're good to go.

BEFORE WORKING A KNIT STITCH, MAKE SURE THE YARN IS POSITIONED BEHIND THE NEEDLES.

If your circular needle's cable is unbearably twisty, let it sit for a couple of minutes in a bath of hot water. This relaxes the cable and makes it much more cooperative.

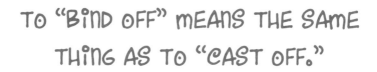

TO "BIND OFF" MEANS THE SAME
THING AS TO "CAST OFF."

Consider using circular needles when knitting in tight quarters. No more jabbing your neighbor with the ends of your straight needles.

A SWEATER DRYING RACK MAKES
AN EXCELLENT BLOCKING SURFACE
FOR FINISHED GARMENTS OR OTHER
KNITTED PROJECTS.

Speed up blocking time by positioning the dampened, blocked piece beneath a ceiling fan or close to a heating or cooling vent.

Sort your yarn remnants by color and splice
them together to create a beautiful palette of hues.
Or forget color schemes altogether and tie on
what you blindly grab from the pile. Whatever you
knit from your "new" multicolored yarn
will definitely be one-of-a-kind.

NEEDLES, YARN, A FIRE IN THE HEARTH—HEAVEN AWAITS.

SANDY BEERS

Use rust-proof pins to block damp garments or lace. To purchase these pins, check the sewing department of your favorite store, or order from a magazine or online venue.

TRY A SLIP-STITCH PATTERN TO CREATE DECORATIVE DESIGNS ON COZY MITTENS, SOCKS, OR SCARVES.

If you'd like to learn a new technique but don't have access to a tutor, you can find plenty of how-to videos on various knitting and social Web sites. Or, purchase instructive DVDs that allow you to replay the steps and tips until you've mastered the technique.

Once upon a time, knitters learned fancy stitches and patterns by studying knitting samplers. Samplers were long strips of knitting divided into sections with each section devoted to a different stitch or pattern. The advent of printed patterns made knitting samplers obsolete.

WHEN YOU KNIT IN THE ROUND,
THE RIGHT SIDE OF THE WORK
IS ALWAYS FACING YOU.

Don't fear the short-row. This shaping technique is simple once you get started. Knit partway across a row; turn the work leaving the unworked stitches on the needle, and purl back the way you came. Follow the pattern directions to make sure your short-rows turn out as expected.

KNITTED SHAWLS STAY PUT WHEN DRAPED AROUND THE SHOULDERS AND FASTENED WITH A DECORATIVE SHAWL PIN. FOR A WHIMSICAL TOUCH, SLIP A KNITTING NEEDLE THROUGH THE SHAWL AND POP A POINT PROTECTOR ON THE END.

When you finish a project, drop your yarn label, leftover yarn, and gauge swatch into a plastic zip-top bag. Store the bag in an easily accessible location. This way if you need to make repairs, you'll have the extra yarn on standby. Laundering directions will be handy, too.

To slip a marker, work your way to it and then slide it from the left-hand needle to the right-hand needle. Continue working until the next marker and then repeat the action.

*Whatever your hand finds to do,
do it with all your might.*

ECCLESIASTES 9:10

Help preserve the ribbed edging of items knit from non-resilient yarns like cotton or ramie by running a thin elastic thread through the back side of a few rows of rib stitches.

IF YOU DISLIKE KNITTING FROM CHARTS, WRITE OUT THE PATTERN ROW BY ROW.

Floats are the lengths of yarn that
are carried across the back of a piece of
Fair Isle or stranded knitting.

WHEN KNITTING IN THE ROUND,
ALL THE YARN ENDS WILL BE
ON THE INSIDE OF THE WORK.

TO GET THE HANG OF WORKING WITH
A CABLE NEEDLE, PRACTICE ON SMALL
PROJECTS LIKE HEADBANDS OR SCARVES.
SAVE YOUR BEST PRACTICE PIECES TO
GIVE AS GIFTS.

Remember that "oops!" moment when you realized you'd just purchased your tenth pair of 14-inch size 8 needles? Put the brakes on duplicate purchases by taking a list of the sizes and lengths of all your knitting needles with you when you go shopping.

If you're not comfortable knitting with a row counter on the needle, slip the counter onto a length of scrap yarn and wear it around your neck.

REVERSIBLE PATTERNS LOOK THE SAME ON BOTH SIDES AND ARE ESPECIALLY NICE FOR SCARVES OR SHAWLS.

Knitting perfectly matched sleeves is a breeze if you cast them both onto the same needle, using a separate ball of yarn per sleeve. Work across the needle, dropping the yarn from one sleeve before picking up for the other.

TIME—SUCH A PRECIOUS
GIFT IS IT;
TO WORK, TO READ,
AND YES, TO KNIT.

MINNIE GERTZ

POINTIER NEEDLES ARE MORE CONVENIENT WHEN KNITTING CABLES OR LACE BECAUSE THEY ARE EASIER TO INSERT INTO THE YARN.

Don't relegate sock yarn to the sock drawer. Knit up a baby sweater, cap, or mittens from comfy sock yarn and prepare to pamper your favorite gift recipient.

MANY YARN COMPANY WEB SITES
OFFER FREE KNITTING PATTERNS AND
CREATIVE CRAFT IDEAS.

To knit a sweater or cardigan with minimal finishing requirements, cast on a top-down pattern. These patterns are knit in the round from the neck down using circular needles for the body and sleeves and double-pointed needles for the cuffs.

Toss a little technology into your knitting bag by trying an electronic row counter. There is even a model that keeps track of rows, repeats, and stitches all at once.

KNITTED BOOK COVERS, CELL PHONE TOTES, OR LAPTOP COZIES MAKE GREAT GIFTS FOR THE PERSON WHO HAS EVERYTHING.

If your stockinette stitch scarf curls along the edges, there's nothing wrong with your knitting. This obstinate behavior is normal for stockinette stitch.

USE UP SOME OF THOSE ODDBALL YARN REMNANTS BY KNITTING THEM INTO STYLISH I-CORD HAIR RIBBONS, PACKAGE TIES, DRAWSTRINGS, OR SIMPLE BELTS.

Miniature knitted sweaters, caps,
or socks make charming decorations
for packages or holiday displays.

HONEY, HAVE YOU EVER SEEN
A MAN KNITTING SOCKS?

Ezer Weizman

Second Sock Syndrome is a common affliction among knitters. Symptoms include knitting one sock of a pair, setting it aside, and starting another project without knitting the second sock. Fortunately, this ailment can be cured by learning to knit two socks at once on long circular needles.

Yarn labels can be fabulous sources of free knitting patterns. You'll find anything from blankets to sweaters, from dishcloths to toys, hats, scarves, and socks. Check the label for a picture of the item; detailed instructions will be printed on the inside.

Woolgathering is the act of shopping for, drooling over, and purchasing yarn for knitting purposes. This is not to be confused with the other type of woolgathering, which refers to daydreaming, though there are remarkable similarities.

NAB A FEW OF THOSE FREE TOTE BAGS OFFERED AT CONFERENCES. THEY MAKE FINE KNITTING BAGS.

K2P2 ribbing is the same thing as 2x2 ribbing. Both abbreviations mean that you should knit two stitches, purl two stitches, alternating between the two sets of stitches until you reach the end of the row.

SPLIT STITCH MARKERS CAN BE PULLED OPEN AND MOVED AS NEEDED FROM PLACE TO PLACE AMONG THE STITCHES.

Thrums are bits of yarn or roving (unspun sheep's wool) knitted along with the working yarn. The strum ends hang out on the wrong side of the work, forming a cozy, insulating layer inside mittens or other garments where you need extra warmth.

For a fun change of pace in sock knitting, cast on one of the toe-up patterns. No toe seams are necessary, as the toe is finished as you go. And fitting is easy because you can try on the sock body as you work.

IF PART OF A PATTERN CONFUSES YOU,
TAKE A LITTLE TIME TO PUZZLE THROUGH
IT AND FIGURE OUT EXACTLY WHAT
YOU NEED TO DO. THEN WRITE OUT THE
CONFUSING PARTS IN A WAY THAT MAKES
SENSE TO YOU AND KNIT ON!

Diligent hands will rule.

PROVERBS 12:24

Some shawl or scarf patterns tell you to knit until you've used up a specified number of yarn skeins. By using the recommended amounts, your garment will be the expected length. However, you can easily adjust the size by using more or less yarn than the stated amount.

Many knitters claim to have spotted a UFO. But don't worry about their sanity; chances are that you've seen a UFO, too, and may even have one or more in your possession! (Hint: UFO is knitter's shorthand for UnFinished Object.)

SMALL CABLES CAN BE WORKED
WITHOUT USING A CABLE NEEDLE;
FIND EASY-TO-FOLLOW TUTORIALS
ON THE WEB.

Before picking up stitches for the first time, practice on a swatch. This will help you avoid clumsy or frayed stitches on that cardigan you spent so many hours knitting.

Wash and dry your knitted sample swatches in the same manner you intend to launder your finished item, checking for any possible changes in the fabric following cleaning. It's better to spoil the swatch than to ruin your precious garment.

YOU KNOW YOU'RE A KNITTER WHEN WATCHING A MOVIE CHARACTER KNIT MAKES YOU ALL TINGLY.

Knitting needles with lighted tips are perfect for those times when you want to knit in a dimly lit public place, such as a movie theater.

DROPPED STITCHES AREN'T ALWAYS MISTAKES. SOME PATTERNS FEATURE THEM AS DESIGN ELEMENTS.

Check the WPI, or wraps per inch, before substituting yarns. Wrap a length of yarn around a ruler to cover one inch, making sure that the wraps lie neatly side by side without crowding. Yarns with similar WPI measurements make suitable substitutes for each other.

HEIRLOOM IS KNITTING CODE FOR
"THIS PATTERN IS SO DIFFICULT THAT YOU
WOULD CONSIDER DEATH A RELIEF."

STEPHANIE PEARL-MCPHEE

WHEN YOU GIVE THE GIFT OF A
HAND-KNITTED ITEM, YOU'RE GIVING
AWAY A LITTLE PIECE OF YOUR HEART.

KNITTED SHOPPING BAGS ARE GREAT
REUSABLE ALTERNATIVES TO
PLASTIC OR PAPER BAGS.

Keep a few squares of heavy cardboard (pieces cut from cereal boxes work great) in your knitting bag. These come in handy for the times when you need to whip up a few pompoms, tassels, or fringe.

BOLD, BRIGHT MULTICOLORED OR VARIEGATED YARNS CAN OBSCURE STITCH PATTERNS. TO MAKE YOUR PRETTY PATTERN STITCHES POP, CHOOSE SOLID COLORED YARNS.

ONE HUNDRED PERCENT COTTON YARN ISN'T A GOOD CHOICE FOR SOCK KNITTING, AS IT ISN'T PLIANT ENOUGH TO PROVIDE A COMFY FIT.

Strive to make each item you knit better than the last. Who knows? The next wedding gift or baby layette may become a treasured family heirloom.

Simple tips…just for knitters.

This collection of inspiration and must-have knitting tips will provide you with what you need to stitch together a beautiful pattern for everyday living.

ISBN 978-1-61626-224-2

EAN

9 781616 262242

50599

>

Religion / Inspirational

DAYMAKER™
INSPIRATIONAL GIFTS